SPACE

Pam Spence

Miranda

A Golden Photo Guide from St. Martin's Press

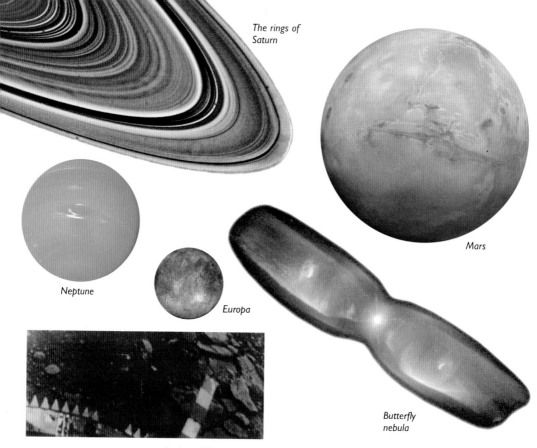

The rings of
Saturn

Mars

Neptune

Europa

Butterfly
nebula

Surface of Venus

SPACE

A Golden Photo Guide from St. Martin's Press

Earth from space

St. Martin's Press
New York

Manufactured in China

Produced by
Elm Grove Books Limited
Series Editor Susie Elwes
Text Editor Angela Wilkes
Art Director Susi Martin
Index Hilary Bird
Picture Research
Joanne Beardwell
Digital Illustration Chris Taylor

Original Edition © 2000 Image Quest
Limited
This edition © 2001
Elm Grove Books Limited

St. Martin's Press
175 Fifth Avenue
New York N.Y.10010.
www.stmartins.com

A CIP catalogue record for this
book is available from the
Library of Congress

ISBN 1-58238-178-X

Text and Photographs in this
book previously published in
Eyewitness 3D Space

This edition published 2001

Acknowledgements
Ecoscene/Gryniewicz 21BR; **Alan Fitzsimmons** 35BL; **Galaxy Picture Library** 15BCL, 19TL, 19BR, 19TR, 31TL/ Michael Stecker 35TC; **Genesis Space Photo Library** 5BC, 7BR, 11BL(inset), 13BL, 17CL, 17BR, 23BR, 33TL, 43BR, 45TL; **Robert Harding Picture Library** 5BL, 11TL, 27BR, /A T Kamajian 35TR, 49BL, 53BL (inset); **Image Select/**Ann Ronan 43C, Index; **NASA** Title & Contents pages, 5TR, 7TR, 9TC, 9TR, 11BR, 17B, 19B, 21BL, 21TR, 23TR, 23C, 25T, 25B, 29T, 29BL, 31B, 31TR, 31C, 33B, 33T, 35TL, 37C, 39T, 39B, 41TR, 45TR, Index, /HST 49BR; **Novosti** (London) 5TL; **Oxford Scientific Films**/Nick Gordon 9BR; **Royal Observatory, Edinburgh** 41BC; **Science Photo Library** 13BC, 17TR, 37BC, 43TR, 51BR, /Dr Alcock 41BL, /Arizona State University 45BC, /Celestial Image Co 45TC, 47BL, 49TL, /CNES 11BL, /Lynette Cook 53BR, /Luke Dodd 45BR, /David Ducros 13TR, /Dr England 37TL, /D Ermakoff/Eurelios 41TL, Index /ESA 13TC, 13BR, /Fred Espenak 23TC, /John Foster 37TR, /George Holton 9BCL, /Steven Jay 35BC, /J Lodriguss 37BR, /NASA 7B, 7TC, 11TR, 11BR(inset), 15BL, 17TL, 23BL, 27BL, 29BR, 37BL, 41BR, 43BL, 45BL, 51BC, 53bc, /Novosti 5TC, 13TL, 35BR, /NRAU/AUI 47TC, /David Parker 5BR /Pekka Parviainen 9BC, /Photo Library International 9TL, /PLI 11TC, /Detlev van Ravenswaay 27BC, /Rev Ronald Royer 15BR, /Royal Observatory Edinburgh 43CL, /John Sandford 43TL, / SETI Institute 53BCR, /Seth Shostak 53TR, /STSI/NASA 47BC, 47BR, /US Geological Survey 25BL, /Frank Zullo 15TC; **Pam Spence** 23BC.

CONTENTS

Saturn

Footprint
on the Moon

INTO SPACE

The exploration of space over the last 50 years has changed our view of the Earth and the Universe. Now the Space Shuttle regularly takes astronauts into space, but only into Earth orbit: a tiny step away from our parent planet. Space is also explored with telescopes and robotic missions to other planets.

SPUTNIK 1
The first unmanned spacecraft placed in Earth orbit was Sputnik 1, launched on October 4, 1957. It took 93 minutes to orbit the Earth. Sputnik 1 burned up in the Earth's atmosphere 92 days later.

FIRST MAN ON THE MOON
Neil Armstrong was the first person to walk on another body in the Solar System. He and his fellow Apollo 11 astronaut, Buzz Aldrin, stepped out onto the Moon in July 1969. Since the Apollo missions, no one has stood on any other body.

UP AND AWAY

To escape from Earth a spacecraft has to reach the speed of at least 7 miles (11.2 km) per second. Any slower, and the craft will fall back to Earth.

The Shuttle is launched into space from Cape Canaveral, Florida.

FIRST SPACEMAN

The first man in space, Yuri Gagarin, made a complete orbit of Earth in Vostok 1 on April 12, 1961. He died test-flying a jet in 1968.

LUNAR MODULE

The Apollo astronauts landed on the Moon's surface in the Lunar Module. An explosion on Apollo 13 crippled the spacecraft and the three astronauts moved into the cramped Lunar Module to use its power to orbit the Moon and return to Earth.

ARIANE

A modern rocket like the European Space Agency's Ariane is smaller than the huge early rockets. Rockets are used to send all kinds of satellites into space. Unlike the Shuttle, they cannot be used again.

esa

LIVING IN SPACE

The visor protects the astronaut's eyes from the glare of the Sun.

Small rocket thrusters enable astronauts to move around.

For humans, space is an alien environment. To live and work in space, people have to carry their own air to breathe, and be protected from extremes of temperature; it is very cold in space, but in the direct rays of the Sun it can also be very hot. All food and power have to be taken on board or generated. Special techniques are needed to cope with weightlessness in space.

EXPERIMENTS

Many experiments have been done to discover how to make best use of the clean and weightless environment of space. It is easier, for example, to make some medicines in space.

SPACE TOILET
For use in zero gravity.

REPAIRS IN SPACE
Astronauts sometimes have to repair equipment orbiting the Earth. The equipment is weightless, so is easy to move, but it is hard doing delicate work in a bulky space suit.

Solar panels generate power.

Repairing the Hubble Space Telescope.

KEEPING FIT
In zero gravity astronauts' muscles don't need to work so hard. To keep fit in space, they must exercise.

EATING
Enough food must be taken into space to last the mission. It has to be stored safely, sometimes for quite a long time. Astronauts also take vitamin supplements.

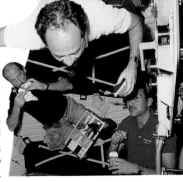

THE EARTH

Our home planet, the Earth, is like a spaceship carrying us in orbit around the Sun. Together with its air and food supply, it has an average speed of 67,000 mph (100,000 km/h), taking one year to complete one solar orbit. The Earth rotates once on its axis every 24 hours, giving us night and day.

The huge oceans make Earth look blue.

Water is frozen at the North and South Poles and forms ice caps.

MELTING ICE

Seventy-one percent of the surface of the Earth is covered by water. Life needs water to survive, but if the Earth heats up very slightly, all the water contained in the ice caps at the poles of the Earth will melt and flood large areas of land worldwide.

THE ATMOSPHERE

The Earth's atmosphere, the air that we breathe, is important for life. As well as giving us oxygen, it blankets the Earth and keeps us warm. It also protects us from the harmful rays of the Sun.

OZONE HOLE

High in the atmosphere of the Earth is the ozone layer. Ozone is a gas that absorbs harmful energy from the Sun. Pollution from cars and industry has started to destroy the ozone layer, making a "hole" in it.

EARTH'S NEIGHBOR

The Moon is 240,000 miles (380,000 km) away from Earth. If you travel at 100 mph (160 km/h), it would take you 100 days to reach the Moon.

The Earth as seen by the Apollo astronauts as they orbited the Moon.

AURORA BOREALIS

The northern (and southern) lights are caused by particles from the Sun spiraling into Earth's atmosphere and reacting with the air. Auroras are most often seen near the poles.

RAIN FORESTS

The oxygen in our air is produced by plants on land and algae in the sea. Continual destruction of huge forests has started to affect the delicate balance of gases in the atmosphere.

9

SATELLITES

When rockets could be built with enough power to escape the pull of the Earth's gravity, it became possible to send different craft into orbit. Spacecraft traveling around the Earth are called satellites, and they have a huge number of uses. Some look down on the Earth, some look out into space, and others bounce radio and television signals around the world.

TELSTAR
The Telstar series were early communications satellites. Telstar I carried the first live transatlantic television broadcast.

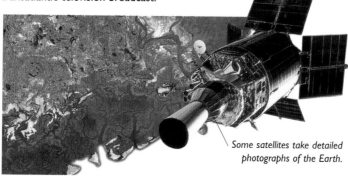

Some satellites take detailed photographs of the Earth.

SPY SATELLITES
Some satellites look back down on Earth and can see in such detail that they are used to monitor troop movements during wars. Other satellites monitor precious Earth resources and help geologists to understand the structure of our planet. These satellites can give warning of natural disasters such as volcanic eruptions.

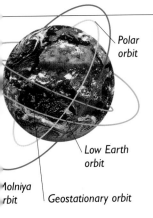

Polar orbit

Low Earth orbit

Molniya orbit

Geostationary orbit

INTERNATIONAL SPACE STATION
Many nations are working together to build a new space station where people will live and work. This space station will continue the work started by the first Russian-designed space station, MIR.

The solar cells use the sunlight for power.

EARTH ORBITS
Satellites follow different orbits depending on the job they are doing. Satellites in geostationary orbit stay over the same part of the Earth's surface. Most communications satellites are in geostationary orbits.

WEATHER SATELLITES
Satellites can monitor Earth's weather from above the clouds. Daily pictures give meteorologists information about storms brewing or the track of a hurricane.

EXPLORING SPACE

Exploring space is dangerous and expensive for astronauts. Since the Apollo program ended, only unmanned spacecraft have been used to explore other bodies in the Solar System. Designs of the landing craft vary, as each explorer spacecraft has to cope with a different range of alien environments – from the incredible pressure and soaring temperatures of Venus to the almost non existent pull of gravity at the surface of a comet.

LUNOKHOD
Eight-wheeled unmanned Soviet vehicles roamed the surface of the Moon, taking photographs and soil samples.

APOLLO ROVER
The Lunar Rover is the only vehicle that has carried astronauts across the surface of another body in the Solar System. It was used on three Apollo missions and enabled the astronauts to explore far more of the lunar surface than if they had just been on foot.

Parachutes will slow the Huygens probe down.

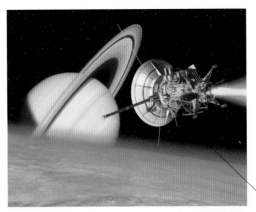

CASSINI MISSION
The Cassini spacecraft, launched in 1997, carries the Huygens probe. This is designed to plunge through the atmosphere of Saturn's moon, Titan, and land on its surface, which may have lakes of liquid methane.

Cassini will take seven years to reach Saturn.

ROSETTA MISSION
The Rosetta orbiter will chase the comet Wirtanen for two years as it rushes toward the Sun. A lander from the orbiter will attach itself to the comet's frozen core and analyze samples from it.

VIKING MISSION
The first craft to land on the surface of Mars were the Viking probes. Two probes landed in 1976 and sent back data and pictures.

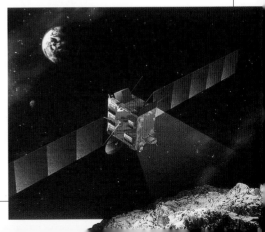

THE SUN

The Sun is a star. Over one million Earths could fit into the Sun, but even with this vast size it is a relatively small star. A star shines with its own light: it produces all of its energy by nuclear fusion. At the center of the Sun, hydrogen is being changed into helium, and the temperature is 15 million degrees kelvin. The energy produced radiates out into space. The Sun supplies all of the energy needed for life on Earth.

In X-ray light, bright solar flares can be seen where sunspots lie. The dark patches are called coronal holes.

SUN SPOTS

In ordinary light, dark spots can be seen on the photosphere of the Sun. These are sunspots. The number of sunspots visible indicates how active the Sun is; at times of greatest solar activity, it produces a lot of solar flares and many sunspots will appear.

STARRY SKY

The Sun is an ordinary star, one of millions in a huge group of stars called a galaxy. It looks bigger than the other stars because it is much closer to us. Stars farther away are seen as points of light.

ECLIPSE OF THE SUN

Sometimes the Moon passes between the Sun and Earth and blocks the Sun's ordinary light, giving us a chance to see the corona.

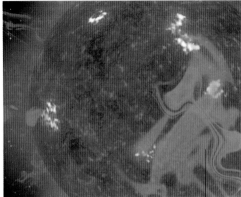

A solar flare can extend more than ten times longer than the diameter of the Earth.

SOLAR POWER HOUSE

The Sun is the most powerful object in our Solar system. One solar flare can produce as much energy as America uses in ten years.

The Sun's outer atmosphere, the corona.

Partial eclipse

Baily's beads

Diamond ring

THE SOLAR SYSTEM

About four and a half billion years ago, a huge rotating cloud of dust and gas in space collapsed. As it collapsed it grew hotter, and eventually the center became so hot that nuclear fusion began, turning the hydrogen into helium. This was the birth of our Sun. As the outer dust cloud cooled, the planets began to form.

DISTANCES FROM THE SUN

The Earth is the third planet from the Sun. Pluto is the farthest planet from the Sun except when its orbit passes inside Neptune.

The Sun is the biggest object in the Solar System.

1 2 3 4

SHOEMAKER LEVY COMET

In 1994, the comet Shoemaker Levy-9 was pulled close to Jupiter. It broke up under Jupiter's tug and slammed into the giant planet.

SHOEMAKER LEVY IMPACT

The impacts of comet Shoemaker Levy-9 were seen from Earth, even by astronomers with fairly small telescopes. The comet fragments disappeared into Jupiter's clouds, but dark marks showed for several days.

5

Young star

NEW SOLAR SYSTEMS

It is only recently that telescopes have been powerful enough to see disks of dust and gas around young stars forming new solar systems.

HORSEHEAD NEBULA

Between the stars lie huge clouds of dust and gas from which, sometimes, solar systems are formed. The Horsehead Nebula is a dark cloud silhouetted against another cloud that has been heated up by newly born stars.

MOON CRATERS

When the Solar System was young, there was a lot of left-over rocks and ice. Some crashed into the planets and their moons. Because our Moon has no atmosphere or weather, these impact craters have not been worn away.

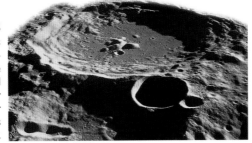

HOW MANY MILLION MILES FROM THE SUN?

1. Mercury: 36
2. Venus: 67
3. Earth: 93
4. Mars: 140
5. Jupiter: 480
6. Saturn: 890
7. Uranus: 1,780
8. Neptune: 2,800
9. Pluto: 3,670

6   7   8   9

MERCURY AND VENUS

Mercury and Venus lie closer to the Sun than the Earth. Mercury is a barren little world. Venus is almost the same size as Earth, and it was once believed to be a tropical paradise. Instead it turned out to be a tropical hell, with searing temperatures, immense atmospheric pressure that would crush you to a pulp, and a poisonous atmosphere with acid rain.

MERCURY

The closest planet to the Sun is a lifeless, cratered world with little atmosphere. The daytime temperature reaches hundreds of degrees kelvin, while at night the temperature plunges below freezing.

PANCAKE DOMES

Strange, circular domelike hills can be seen on Venus. They are thought to be the result of thick eruptions of lava from vents on flat land. They have only been seen on Venus.

The Alpha Regio region imaged by the Magellan spacecraft.

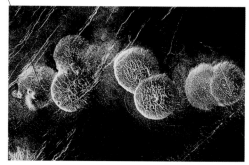

VOLCANIC LANDSCAPE

It is impossible to see through the thick clouds surrounding Venus, but the Magellan spacecraft used radar to image the surface. It found it was covered by volcanoes of all sizes and huge lava plains. It is not known if any of the volcanoes are still active.

A computer-generated image of the surface of Venus from Magellan data.

EVENING STAR

Venus is often a brilliant object in the evening sky, giving rise to its popular name.

A Magellan radar image of Venus shows the highland region, Aphrodite Terra, sprawling across the planet.

PROBING THE SURFACE

The Venera probes were sent to study Venus. Some of them made it through the crushing atmosphere to the surface, from where they sent back data and images.

POISONOUS CLOUDS

The thick clouds covering Venus consist mostly of carbon dioxide. These clouds trap the Sun's rays, which then heat the surface to high temperatures.

PLANET EARTH

The third planet from the Sun, the Earth, is the only planet with large oceans of liquid water. The oceans absorb carbon dioxide from the atmosphere, as do plants. Green plants give off oxygen, helping to create the air we can breathe. Earth's atmosphere helps to keep the surface of the planet warm, and protects it from harmful radiation from the Sun.

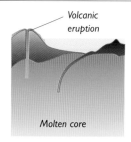

Volcanic eruption

Molten core

MOVING PLATES

The Earth is made up of layers of material, from the hot molten core to the rocky outer crust. Its outer layer, the lithosphere, is broken into a number of plates that move about an inch each year.

MOUNTAINS

Where two continental plates collide, the Earth's crust is pushed up. The edges of the collision are where mountains such as the Himalayas are formed.

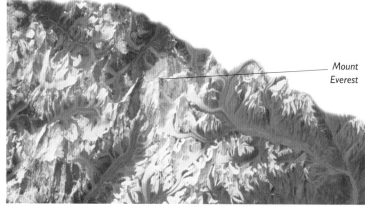

Mount Everest

VOLCANO

The inside of the Earth is very hot, so hot that metal and rock melt to form magma. Magma can force its way to the surface and erupt as volcanic lava, usually where the Earth's surface is already fractured.

The eruption of the Kliuchevskoi volcano was photographed from the Space Shuttle.

AFRICAN RIFT VALLEY

Rift valleys occur when huge long blocks of the Earth's crust sink. Some valleys stretch for thousands of miles. The East African Rift Valley System stretches from halfway along the east side of Africa, through the Red Sea, and as far as the Dead Sea.

LIVING ON VOLCANOES

Many volcanoes erupt along ridges in the seabed. The magma can rise above the sea water and form islands such as Hawaii.

Hot volcanic material pours into the sea.

The wide valley floor of the African Rift Valley.

THE MOON

The Moon is the Earth's only natural satellite. It orbits the Earth at an average distance of 240,000 miles (380,000 km). It is a barren world with almost no atmosphere and no life. The surface of the Moon is pitted with craters made millions of years ago when meteors crashed into it. It also has dark areas of hard volcanic lava known as maria, meaning "sea."

Waxing moon *First quarter*

SILVER MOON

The Moon rotates in the same time it takes to go around the Earth, so the same side of it is always facing us. The bright crater at the bottom is Tycho, the large lava plain on the left-hand side is the Ocean of Storms, Oceanus Procellarum.

DEEP VALLEYS

A long winding valley (Vallis Shröteri) leads between two craters, Aristarchus and Herodotus. The valley looks like a dried-up riverbed.

Tycho has a bright ray system.

The Sea of Tranquillity where Apollo 11 landed.

noon　　　　　*Waning moon*

PHASES OF THE MOON

The Moon seems to
change shape because we
only see the parts of it
that are lit by the Sun.
At "new moon" it
is invisible.

The first person on the
Moon, Neil Armstrong,
is one of just 12 people
who have walked on
the Moon. The last
astronaut left in 1972.

*The hill Hadley Delta
looms behind the
Apollo 15 base.*

SOUTH POLE

The Clementine
probe found
possible traces of
water ice at the
South Pole of the
Moon. The ice lies
at the bottom of
deep craters where
sunlight cannot melt it.

FOOTPRINT ON THE MOON

Neil Armstrong's footprint was made
in July 1969. There is no wind or rain
on the Moon to remove it.

MARS

Mars is often called the red planet since it looks red in the night sky. This is because the rocks and dust on Mars contain a large amount of iron, which gives them a rusty red color. Dust storms often completely conceal the surface of Mars, which has many features that show the effects of strong winds.

A gigantic canyon, the Valles Marineris extends for 2,800 miles (4,500 km).

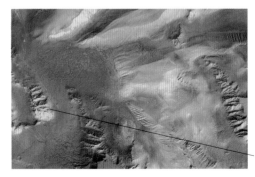

Some features resemble dried-up riverbeds.

ICY POLES
Water ice exists at the Martian poles. Rivers may have existed in the past, but the temperatures and pressures at the surface are too low for liquid water to exist today.

HILLS AND VALLEYS
The northern part of Mars is covered by low-lying plains. The southern hemisphere is very heavily cratered and dotted with mountains and ancient volcanoes.

MARS PATHFINDER

It was once thought that there might have been life on Mars, but probes, including the Pathfinder Mission, discovered a dry, dusty, lifeless world. Nothing lives there today. It is possible very primitive bacteria existed there once, but not the intelligent beings of science fiction stories.

The landing site on Mars shows the planet's surface to be a stony desert.

MOONS

Mars has two small, potato-shaped moons, Phobos and Deimos, which are probably captured asteroids.

Phobos, the largest Martian moon, has a huge crater.

Deimos is only about 9 miles (15 km) across.

OLYMPUS MONS

The largest volcano in the Solar System, Olympus Mons, is about 16 miles (26 km) high and about 370 miles (600 km) across at its base. It is about 200 million years old.

The top of Olympus Mons is 55 miles (90 km) wide.

MARTIAN POLES

In winter, the poles of Mars are covered in water ice and frozen carbon dioxide. In summer, the ice melts.

ASTEROIDS

After the planets were formed, there were still some chunks of rock left orbiting the Sun. Between Mars and Jupiter lies the asteroid belt, a concentration of some of this debris – small, irregular-shaped rocks, hurtling around in orbit. Other asteroids travel closer to the Earth.

The model of the asteroid Toutatis shows how it tumbles over and over as it orbits the sun

ROTATING ASTEROID
Most asteroids slowly rotate, but Toutatis has a strange tumbling motion. Toutatis' orbit occasionally crosses that of the Earth.

Most asteroids have small craters.

IDA AND DACTYL
The Galileo spacecraft, traveling to Jupiter in 1993, took pictures of the asteroid Ida as it passed, and discovered it had a small moon, now called Dactyl. Dactyl is about 60 miles (100 km) from Ida and is only just over 0.62 mile (1 km) across. The largest asteroid is over 560 miles (900 km) across.

Dactyl

RING AROUND THE SUN

Many asteroids orbit the Sun between Mars and Jupiter. This part of the Solar System is known as the asteroid belt. Over 5,000 asteroids have had their orbits calculated.

Rocks of all shapes and sizes make up the asteroid belt.

SIKHOTE-AL METEORITE

Rocky debris that reaches the Earth's surface are called meteorites. Small debris are completely burned up as they pass through the Earth's atmosphere.

ARIZONA CRATER

One of the best-known craters on Earth is the Barringer, or Meteor Crater, in Arizona. It is about 7.5 miles (12 km) wide. It was formed about 25,000 years ago.

JUPITER

Jupiter is the largest and most massive planet in the Solar System. On its own it weighs more than all of the other planets together. It is mainly composed of hydrogen and helium. Violent storms rage in its atmosphere, where wind speeds can reach 500 miles (800 km) per hour at the edges of the cloud belts. Its orange and yellow coloring is probably due to traces of elements such as sulfur.

THE GREAT RED SPOT

One of the most famous and visible features of Jupiter is the Great Red Spot. It varies in size, but is often larger than the diameter of the Earth. It is a huge rotating weather system and has been observed for over 300 years, ever since records began.

THE GALILEAN MOONS

Jupiter has 16 known moons. The four largest are known as the Galilean moons because they were first seen by Galileo in 1610. They are easily visible as points of light through small telescopes or binoculars.

Callisto   *Ganymede*

Observed from Earth, the Galilean moons' positions change day by day as they orbit Jupiter.

JUPITER'S RINGS

In 1979 a thin ring system was discovered around Jupiter. The rings are made of small particles of rock and ice.

JUPITER THE GIANT

If Jupiter were on one side of a pair of scales and all of the other planets were on the other side, Jupiter would be heavier. Its diameter is 12 times that of the Earth.

One of Jupiter's moons passes in front of the giant planet.

Europa

Io

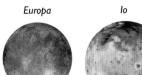

JUPITER'S PULL

Io is the nearest Galilean moon to Jupiter and it is constantly being pulled by Jupiter's gravity. This heats up Io's core, creating active volcanoes.

Active volcano

MISSION TO JUPITER

The Galileo spacecraft arrived at Jupiter in 1995. It launched a probe into Jupiter's clouds and sent back detailed pictures of the Galilean moons.

SATURN

One of the most beautiful planets is Saturn, with its large ring system visible from Earth through binoculars or a small telescope. Saturn is a "gas giant" like Jupiter, mainly composed of hydrogen and helium. Since it is farther from the Sun than Jupiter, it is also cooler. Saturn's clouds form at a lower level than Jupiter's, so the planet's bands and spots are less visible.

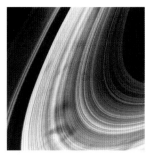

RADIAL SPOKES
Close scrutiny of some pictures show strange dark bands radiating out across the rings. It is thought that these bands are caused by small dust grains.

SATURN'S RINGS
The rings of Saturn were first noted by Galileo in 1610 when he saw "handles" through his small telescope. There are now detailed images of the rings showing they are made up of distinct bands. There are gaps between the bands; the largest is Cassini's division between the A and B rings.

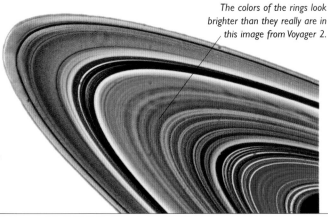

The colors of the rings look brighter than they really are in this image from Voyager 2.

30

ICY RINGS

Saturn's rings are not solid, but are made up of thousands of tiny particles of dust and ice held in place by "shepherd satellites," tiny moons. These push and pull the particles and stop them from escaping.

Saturn's poles are flattened because the planet rotates so fast.

TITAN

Saturn's largest moon is Titan. It is the second-largest moon in the whole Solar System (Jupiter's Ganymede is the largest). Titan is very unusual because it has a dense atmosphere. The Huygens probe has been sent to discover if lakes of liquid methane exist on Titan.

Tethys

Enceladus

The surface of Titan is concealed by its thick atmosphere.

SATURN'S MANY MOONS

There are 18 known moons of Saturn. Six of them are icy and are similar to the three outer Galilean moons of Jupiter; the rest are small and rocky.

URANUS AND NEPTUNE

Uranus was the first planet to be discovered with a telescope. Its slightly irregular orbit suggested the existence of yet another planet and led to the discovery of Neptune. They are both gas giants, composed mainly of hydrogen and helium. Uranus has nine thin rings and Neptune has three twisted rings.

UMBRIEL
Probably Uranus' oldest moon, Umbriel is very heavily cratered.

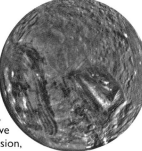

MIRANDA
Miranda, one of Uranus' moons, has a strange, wrinkled surface. It may have been blasted apart by a collision, then re-formed from the debris.

SIDEWAYS AROUND THE SUN
Uranus orbits the Sun spinning on its side, probably as a result of a collision in the past. This means that the planet's poles point toward or away from the Sun for long periods of time, creating the longest seasons in the Solar System.

TRITON

Neptune's largest moon, Triton,was probably a body captured by the planet from the nearby Kuiper belt. It is very similar to Pluto in size and composition.

Neptune rises beyond one of its moons.

GALE FORCE

The winds at the top of Neptune's clouds are among the fastest in the Solar System, traveling at half a mile (700 meters) per second.

BLUE PLANETS

Uranus and Neptune have a distinct blue color. This is due to the traces of methane in their atmospheres. Methane absorbs red light, making everything look blue.

This oval weather system raced around Neptune in 18 hours.

NEPTUNE

The most distant gas giant, Neptune, is slightly smaller than Uranus. It has eight known moons (Uranus has 17) and weather systems that zip around the planet in the high winds, then disappear.

PLUTO AND COMETS

On the edge of the Solar System lies a small, cold, rocky body and thousands of icy lumps of debris. The rocky body is Pluto, the ninth and smallest planet, although some question whether it should be classed as a planet. A huge cloud of icy debris, called the Oort Cloud, surrounds the Solar System. Sometimes lumps of ice are dislodged and plunge, displaying cometary tails, toward the Sun.

PLUTO
Pluto is so far away and so small, it is difficult for even the biggest telescopes to see much detail. This is a computer-generated image taken by the Hubble Space Telescope.

CHARON
Pluto has a moon, Charon, which is more than half its size.

KUIPER BELT
This is a belt of icy, rocky debris lying beyond the orbit of Neptune. Pluto is the largest object in the Kuiper belt.

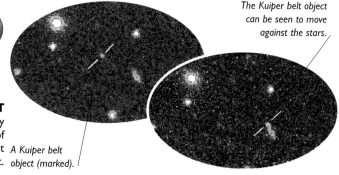

The Kuiper belt object can be seen to move against the stars.

A Kuiper belt object (marked).

ECCENTRIC ORBIT

Pluto is usually the farthest planet from the Sun but its elongated orbit can take it nearer the Sun than Neptune.

An artist's impression of Pluto and Charon

The tail of the comet hides the body.

HALE-BOPP COMET

Some comets can be very spectacular if they pass close to the Earth. Hale-Bopp was a very bright comet clearly visible in 1997.

METEOR SHOWERS

Particles from the debris left by a comet burn up if they enter Earth's atmosphere; this produces meteor showers.

TUNGUSKA EVENT

A gigantic explosion above central Siberia in 1908 flattened trees over a large area. One theory is that this devastation was caused by a small comet hitting the Earth.

TIME AND DISTANCE

From Pluto, the Sun appears only as a very bright star. Light from the Sun takes over five hours to reach Pluto at the edge of the Solar System, an average distance of 4,000 million miles (6,000 million km). A light year is the distance traveled by light in one year. It is about 5.6 million, million miles or 9 million, million kilometers. Light from the Sun in our Solar System takes over 25,000 years to reach the center of our spiral galaxy.

Image of a barred spiral galaxy made by a radio telescope.

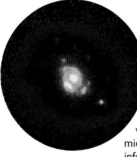

Image of a barred spiral galaxy made using ultraviolet light.

COMPARING SIGNALS

Light is energy that our eyes can detect, but other detectors can "see" in different ways, such as X-ray, microwave, and radio. New information can be learned by looking at an object using a different wavelength.

Blue shift

Red shift

RED AND BLUE SHIFT

If an object is moving away from us, its light is stretched out and appears redder. The red shift can tell us how far away the object lies. The light from an object moving toward us is blue shifted.

THE SUN FROM PLUTO

Pluto lies in the icy outer part of our Solar System and receives little heat or light from the Sun. Humans would find it impossible to live on such a cold world.

The Sun looks like a star from Pluto.

LOOKING BACK

The farthest object we can see is the Andromeda Galaxy. Its light takes over two million years to reach Earth, so we see it as it was two million years ago.

THE REVOLVING SKY

The Earth turns on its axis once a day. At night, this movement makes the stars appear to trace out curved paths through the sky.

PROXIMA CENTAURI

This is the nearest star to our Sun. It is over four light years away, so light from it takes four years to reach us.

The two nearest stars, alpha and Proxima Centauri, orbit each other.

SPACE EYES

The Hubble Space Telescope is an extremely successful modern space telescope. It was launched into orbit around the Earth in April 1990. Positioned beyond Earth's atmosphere where it can see very clearly, it has revolutionized many branches of astronomy by its findings. The Hubble images are used by scientists of all nations.

CLUSTERS OF STARS
Around the disc of our galaxy lie spherical clusters of old stars. These globular clusters look like swarms of bright bees. The Hubble Telescope has managed to image one group in the Andromeda galaxy that is over two million light years away.

SPACE BUTTERFLY
As stars use up their nuclear fuel they expand, losing the outer layers of their atmospheres. This butterfly-shaped nebula, a cloud of stellar material or plasma, is one such dying star. The star's magnetic field pulls the plasma into the butterfly shape.

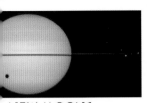

NEW MOONS

As the Earth and Saturn orbit the Sun, the two planets slowly tilt at different angles to each other. We see either the top of Saturn's rings, or we see them edge-on. Hubble discovered more moons when the rings were edge-on.

AN EYE IN SPACE

The Hubble Space Telescope orbits beyond the light pollution and the distortion of Earth's atmosphere. As well as taking optical images it looks at objects in ultraviolet, and near infrared.

Hubble uses solar panels for power.

TARANTULA NEBULA

The star cluster at the bottom right of this Hubble image shows where new stars are forming. It lies in the Tarantula nebula.

INNER SPIRALS

Hubble is able to see features in the nucleus of a giant spiral galaxy that lies tens of millions of light years away from Earth.

BIRTH OF A STAR

Between the stars are vast clouds of dust and gas. If these clouds collapse, dust and gas condense in pockets within the cloud. These pockets can become extremely hot. Some regions become hot enough for nuclear fusion to start: hydrogen is converted to helium and energy is released as light – a star is born.

BETA PICTORIS

A young star, beta Pictoris, has been imaged using infrared light. The main star was blocked out so that the surrounding dust and gas can be seen, forming what is believed to be the new star's solar system.

BROWN DWARF

Small pockets of condensed gas that are not large enough for the their centers to reach nuclear fusion temperature become brown dwarfs. They are more massive than planets, but they are not stars.

Infrared light shows the dust and gas surrounding the young star beta Pictoris.

EAGLE NEBULA

This is a close-up view of the Eagle nebula taken by the Hubble Space Telescope. The finger-shaped tops of this vast cloud of dust and gas are larger than our Solar System. They contain young stars.

Stars are forming in the condensed gas and dust.

STARS IN SPIRALS

In some galaxies, gas and dust are compressed in waves that create new stars. The waves spiral through the galaxies and the newly born, bright stars show up the spiral shape. These galaxies are called spiral galaxies.

THE PLEIADES

This star cluster in the constellation of Taurus contains as many as 3,000 stars. The stars are young, hot, and bright. The blue color is the stars' light reflecting off surrounding dust and gas.

The seven sisters, or Pleiades.

Young hot stars light up the spiral arms of a galaxy.

CONSTELLATIONS

Constellations are patterns of stars we see from Earth. There is often no physical connection between them. One of the most recognizable constellations is Orion, the hunter. His "belt" is represented by three stars, with a "sword" of stars hanging from it. Orion can be seen from most parts of the world. At his feet is Sirius, the brightest star in our sky after the Sun.

Orion, with his belt. and sword is easy to spot.

Lying among the stars of Orion's sword is the Orion nebula.

LOOKING INTO THE ORION NEBULA

The Orion nebula lies over 120 light years away, so we see it as it was 120 years ago. Using larger telescopes, we can see details in the cloud of hot gas and dust, such as four of the new young stars that have formed.

The Trapezium consists of four hot young stars embedded in the Orion nebula.

ORION, THE HUNTER

The ancient Greeks named the constellations after many of their gods. Orion was the son of the sea god Poseidon.

ORION NEBULA

The pinkish glow in Orion's sword, sometimes visible without a telescope, is the light from a large cloud of dust and gas glowing with the heat of new stars.

This old star map shows Orion holding a club; in others he holds a bow.

Betelgeuse is a star that may explode because it is near the end of its life.

ORION

This is the most recognizable part of the constellation of Orion. Orion's shoulders, tunic, belt, and sword are marked out by stars. The bottom right hand star of his tunic is Rigel, a giant blue-white star.

BETELGEUSE

Most stars are so far away that they look like points of light. Betelgeuse is large and fairly near, so it is seen as a disk.

DEATH OF A STAR

When massive stars use up all their energy they explode, blasting their outer layers into space. A giant exploding star is called a supernova, and for a short time it can outshine a galaxy. The remnants of the giant star shrink until it is a small, dense neutron star. Some shrink further and become black holes. Smaller stars, such as the Sun, shrink to become white dwarfs.

PLANETARY NEBULAE

As stars age, they shed their outer layers as "planetary nebulae." These have nothing to do with planets, but they looked like planets to early astronomers.

STINGRAY NEBULA

Many planetary nebulae are pulled into strange and beautiful shapes by the magnetic forces left by the old star. They are sometimes given names like this "stingray" nebula.

The Hourglass planetary nebula.

A dying star makes the dust cloud glow.

DEATH OF A STAR

The dying star Eta Carinae has produced this beautiful nebula. Many stars cast off outer layers as they age, and the star dust is twisted into weird and wonderful shapes. Eta Carinae will probably explode as a supernova.

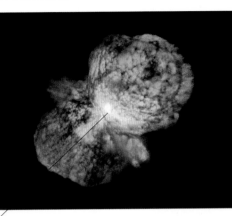

Eta Carinae is a massive star nearing the end of its life.

SUPERNOVA BANG

In 1987, a supernova exploded in the Large Magellanic Cloud. Far left is the supernova before its dramatic explosion.

CRAB NEBULA

A massive star exploded in 1054. The remains of this supernova can be seen today in the constellation of Taurus.

After the explosion a central spinning neutron star, a pulsar, was left.

STAR CLUSTER

Clusters of old stars surround the center of spiral galaxies. Some of these clusters can contain up to a million stars.

BLACK HOLES

A black hole is an incredibly dense part of space, so dense that its gravitational pull is strong enough to stop everything, including light, from escaping. Since we can only see objects by the energy they emit, this means we cannot detect black holes by any ordinary means. We only know they exist because of the way they affect other objects.

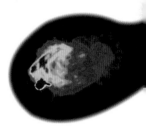

CYGNUS A
Within the constellation of Cygnus is a radio galaxy, with two powerful radio jets. A black hole probably lies at the center of the galaxy.

ACTIVE GALAXIES
Some galaxies are called active galaxies because they send out such a huge amount of energy. They may be eating up smaller galaxies, or they may have a massive black hole at their center, gobbling up stars, dust, and gas. Centaurus A is a large, active galaxy with a dark strip of dust across its middle.

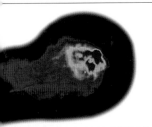

SPINNING MATERIAL

Material spiraling into a black hole takes on a disk shape. It is the energy from these spinning disks that can be detected.

BLACK HOLES

There are two kinds of black holes. Large black holes can exist at the centers of galaxies, causing all kinds of strange effects. Other, smaller, black holes are created when a large massive star, bigger than the Sun, uses up its energy and dies.

Everything near a black hole is pulled toward it and spirals into the black hole from a disk. Sometimes radio jets are ejected.

Material spirals into a black hole in galaxy NGC4261

QUASARS

At the edge of the Universe are quasars: compact, energetic objects with black holes at their centers.

GALAXIES

Our star, the Sun, belongs to a galaxy called the Milky Way – a gigantic spiral of dust, gas, and a hundred thousand million stars. We see it as a band of hazy light across the night sky. The Milky Way belongs to what astronomers call the Local Group, a small cluster of about 30 quite small galaxies. Farther afield are clusters of other galaxies, stretching as far as telescopes can see.

BARRED SPIRAL
Sometimes the spiral arms of a galaxy start from a "bar" of gas, dust, and stars. These "barred" spirals are similar in all other ways to ordinary spirals in which the arms start from a central nucleus.

Massive young stars appear blue in photographs.

SPIRAL GALAXIES
Clouds of dust and gas are sometimes compressed by waves that spiral out from the center and start star formation. The young stars shine brightly, illuminating the spiral structure of the galaxy.

CARTWHEEL GALAXY

A small galaxy that plunged into the center of a large spiral galaxy millions of years ago sends out a shock wave. The "rim" of the cartwheel is this shock wave moving out and compressing the dust and gas as it goes, creating new stars.

Newly formed stars shine brightly.

COLLISION COURSE

The Antennae galaxies are two spiral galaxies that collided about 500 million years ago. The collision created new stars as the dust and gas in the galaxies were compressed.

LARGE MAGELLANIC CLOUD

The nearest galaxy to the Milky Way is the Large Magellanic Cloud, visible from the southern hemisphere. It has an irregular shape because of the gravitational pull of the Milky Way.

THE UNIVERSE

Time, matter, and energy begin.

The Universe is a hot, seething mass, continually cooling and expanding.

After about a minute, protons and neutrons start to form the nuclei of atoms.

The Universe is everything. There is no end to the Universe, no edge or center. It is believed to have started as a Big Bang about 15 billion years ago. Astronomers believe that the Universe is still expanding. Its future depends on how much matter exists. It is impossible to calculate the amount of matter because a lot of it is "dark matter" that cannot be measured.

BIG BANG
The event that created the Universe is called the Big Bang, when everything – time, matter, and space – exploded into existence. Because there is no way of knowing what happened before the Big Bang, it may not be the first or only Big Bang to have happened.

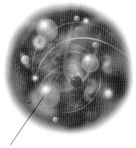

Astronomers estimate that it took a billion years before galaxies formed and stars started to shine.

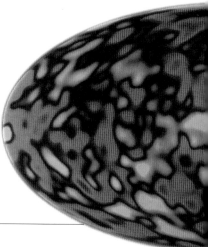

DEEPEST SPACE

The farther away we look, the farther back in time we see. The farthest we have looked is in the Hubble Deep Field, where galaxies are seen as they were when the Universe was only a few billion years old.

Over 3,000 faint galaxies were revealed in the Hubble Deep Field.

GALAXY CLUSTER

The matter in the Universe is not spread out evenly, but is clumped into galaxies. The galaxies are grouped into clusters, and the clusters gather into superclusters around large, empty, bubblelike voids.

SIGNALS FROM THE PAST

In 1964, astronomers discovered a faint background of microwave radio waves. This is the energy left over from the Big Bang, and it is still cooling. The COBE satellite mapped this background

The Virgo cluster has around 2,500 galaxies.

IS ANYBODY OUT THERE?

We know that there is no other intelligent life in our Solar System, but there are so many millions of stars in the Universe that there may be other planets in other solar systems with intelligent life. Some astronomers are listening to the skies, hoping for a signal that would mean we are not alone.

VERY LARGE ARRAY
In New Mexico there is an instrument made up of 27 movable radio antennae on a Y-shaped track. The Very Large Array is one of the best radio telescopes because it can make high-resolution images of radio sources.

ARECIBO DISH

This huge radio telescope "sees" by listening to radio signals. Scientists believe that if other life forms exist in the Universe they will use radio signals that could be heard on Earth.

MINUTE MARTIAN LIFE

There is an ongoing debate as to whether bacteria were found in a Martian meteorite.

A natural hollow near Arecibo, Puerto Rico, is the site of the world's largest radio telescope dish.

SIGNAL

Radio waves come in continually

from all around the galaxy. Computers analyze the data to see if there are any "intelligent" signals among the background noise.

ARECIBO MESSAGE

A message about life on Earth was beamed into space in 1974 from the Arecibo dish.

INDEX

The Sun

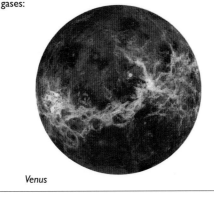

Venus

beta Pictoris

Old star map of Orion

Spiral galaxy